CANTATE DOMINO

A 75th Anniversary Tribute

to the

METHODIST CHURCH MUSIC SOCIETY

1935 - 2010

Compiled and edited by
Godfrey Talford

British Library Cataloguing in Publication Data.
A catalogue record for this book is available
from the British Library.

ISBN 978 086071 650 1

Commissioned Publication of

23 Park Road, Ilkeston, Derbys DE7 5DA
Tel: 0115 932 0643 www.moorleys.co.uk

Contents

This book is dedicated to all former Officers of the Society and to the memory of all those of them who now rejoice with us 'but upon another shore and in a greater light', in recognition of their contributions collectively and individually to its development.

Principal Officers of MCMS

PRESIDENT/CHAIRMAN

Rev Dr F Luke Wiseman	1935-1939
Dr Clifford W Towlson	1939-1963
Rev Dr J Alan Kay	1960-1962*
Rev E Benson Perkins	1962-1967*
Rev Norman P Goldhawk	1965-1983*
Rev Bryan F Spinney	1983-1992
Spencer W Freeman	1992-2000
Rev Nicholas S Young	2000-2006
Spencer W Freeman	2006-2007**
Rev R Graham Tidmarsh	2007-2010

* including a short period as Vice Chairman
** Acting Chair

SECRETARY

Rev Edgar C Barton	1935-1945	
Ronald S Peck	1945-1948	(Lay)
Rev Dr Francis B Westbrook	1945-1975	(Ministerial)
Rev Dr Ivor H Jones	1975-1979	(Ministerial)
Harold G Jones	1948-1974	(Lay)
Miss Margaret Gifford	1974	
Ralph Bailey	1974-1990	(Lay)
Mrs Marion Saunders	1990-1999	
John Bailey	1999-2010	

(In 1983 it was decided to discontinue the post of Ministerial Secretary)

TREASURER

E S Lamplough	1936-1939
William F Redman	1939-1956
Alfred J B Haynes	1945-1955
Ralph K Roundtree	1955-1974
Harold G Jones	1974-1982
Richard H Baker	1982-1987
Rev Tim Pittock	1987-1990
Miss Patricia Rock	1990-1998
Tony Grimley	1998-2002
David Joseph	2002-2004
Tony Grimley	2004
Richard H Baker	2004-2010

Foreword

In its life of seventy-five years, the Methodist Church Music Society (MCMS) has achieved an impressive history. It has provided a service and encouragement to Methodist musicians and, despite a reputation for being 'traditional', has evolved to include the modern developments in church music and the way it is presented for worship.   Who would have thought seventy-five years ago that an MCMS Conference would have included sessions on data projection?!

MCMS has also gone through a number of transitions from being part of the Methodist Connexional Body to being an independent charity alongside the Methodist Church.   During this time too, it was instrumental in the formation of Creative Arts in Methodism (CAM).   Then, when CAM in turn was set loose from the Connexion, it saw a major role in seeking to provide a new home for the Creative Arts.   Thus, as it comes to an end as MCMS and passes the baton to ArtServe, the new body, as for a time did MCMS, seeks to embrace all creative arts for worship.   We wish ArtServe every success in doing so to the glory of God.

Graham Tidmarsh
Chairman of MCMS
September 2010

Acknowledgements

As editor, I acknowledge my indebtedness to all those who have made original contributions to this little book. I have also benefited from the encouragement and support of the Chairman and members of the MCMS Executive Committee in 2009-10. Special thanks are due to Michael Boxall, whose technical help with the reproduction of previously published material has been invaluable, and to Spencer Freeman, who has freely shared with me some of his reminiscences of personalities and proceedings, based on his association with the Society over many more years than mine.

I would also like to acknowledge the sterling work done by Alistair Kennard in drafting an initial Business Plan for ArtServe, which made the task of writing the final chapter so much easier than it would otherwise have been.

Any errors, inconsistencies, or discourtesies are entirely my responsibility and I apologise for them without reservation. It is an immense privilege to have been invited to compile this book—I hope it will be of interest to members of the Society and to members of the churches they have sought to serve.

Godfrey Talford

Contributors

John Bailey is currently Company Secretary of ArtServe. From 1999 to 2010 he was the Secretary/Development Officer of the Methodist Church Music Society, and has been very closely involved with the establishment of ArtServe. A retired Senior Local Government Officer living in Sheffield, he comes from a family of Methodist Organists. For the past 26 years he has been Organist at Endcliffe Methodist Church, Sheffield. He currently holds various positions at Circuit, District and Connexional level, mainly focusing on property related matters.

Barbara Bircumshaw is the Superintendent Minister of the Hinckley Circuit, having previously served as Chair of the North Wales District. She was born in Cardiff and is a lifelong member of the Methodist Church. She first trained as a primary school teacher at Southlands College. She has always been interested in music in worship as a local preacher, a minister and member of the congregation. She has been the Chair of the Methodist Church Music Resources Group since 2004.

Andrew Pratt is a Methodist minister who has written over 600 hymns. He has published a study of the origin of the 1933 Methodist Hymn Book, *'O for a thousand tongues'* (Epworth, 2004), contributed a chapter to *'Charles Wesley, Life Literature and Legacy'* (Epworth 2007) and has written articles for a new Dictionary of Hymnology currently in preparation for publication in the UK and the USA. He has published meditations on Charles Wesley's Hymns, *'Inextinguishable Blaze'* (Inspire, 2007) and served on the Music Resource Group of the Methodist Church from 2004 - 2009. He edits the Bulletin of the Hymn Society of Great Britain and Ireland.

Bryan Spinney was born in Southampton in 1930, where the people and facilities of the newly-built Swaythling Methodist Hall had a profound effect on his life. After joining a Local Preachers' Training Class, he later felt called to the ministry. Trained at Richmond College, he served as a Circuit Minister 1959-95. He joined MCMS in the early 1970s and served as Editor of the *Bulletin* before being elected as the Chairman of the Society. He also served on the Texts Sub-Committee for *Hymns & Psalms*. He has always had an interest in hymns and their tunes and published a reprint of Wesley's *'Foundry Tune Book'* with notes, *'Tuned For Praise'* (Methodist hymnbooks of the 20th Century), and *'Is That The Right Tune?'* (origins and settings of hymn tunes).

Godfrey Talford is a Methodist Local Preacher and principal organist at North Walsham Methodist Church, Norfolk. He served on the MCMS Committee from 2007-10 and edited its magazine, 'NOTES' in 2009-10. He retired from full time employment in 2006 after a career in Human Resources Management in industry and as a General Manager in the charity sector.

The Methodist Church Music Society—a brief history

John Bailey

The inspiration for the Methodist Church Music Society (MCMS) can be traced back to the Methodist Union in 1932, when the former Wesleyan, Primitive and United Methodist Churches combined to form the Methodist Church in Great Britain. One of the first priorities of the united church was to produce a new hymn book for use throughout the Connexion. This was published in December 1933 with the title '*The Methodist Hymn Book*' and is often referred to as the MHB! Within weeks of its publication, Rev Dr W Russell Maltby, a former President of the Wesleyan Church, arranged a retreat for organists and choirmasters at High Leigh, Hoddesdon. This was repeated in January 1935 and led to the formation of a committee which met at City Road, London in March 1935 to found the Methodist Church Music Society.

The following is an extract for the minutes of that committee meeting:

'Minutes of a meeting of the Committee (appointed by the Choirmasters' and Organists' Conference at High Leigh, Hoddesdon in January 1935) held at 25-35 City Road, London, EC1 on Friday March 1st 1935 at 11-30 a.m.

Present Rev F. Luke Wiseman, BA, Chairman; Revs A.S. Gregory, MA; Noel F Hutchcroft, LRAM; Thomas Tiplady; Francis B Westbrook, BA, Mus Doc; W Longon Oakes, BD; Rolan Hind,BA and Edgar C Barton.
Messrs Edmund S Lamplough; C.W Towlson, MA; Fred Wood; R Mountford,FRCO; Fred C Payne; George Baskeyfield, FRCO; Miss Christine Smye, LRAM ABSM; Mrs Grosvenor, Messrs Charles Warner; N.A Rutter; Harold C Walker; G Edward Miles, FRCO, Mus Doc; W F Redman.

Apologies Revs W R Maltby, D D Bertram and E Woods.

The recommendations of the Sub Committee were submitted and the following Constitution was agreed:

Title: That the organisation shall be known as 'The Methodist Church Music Society.

Aim: To cultivate and co-ordinate all the musical resources of Methodism in the service of public worship.

Membership: membership of the Society shall be open to Choirmasters, Organists, Choristers, Ministers and members of the Methodist Church interested in church music.

Methods:

1. An Annual Conference.

2. Sectional Conferences and Local Fraternals.

3. The official organ shall be 'The Choir' Magazine.

4. The formation of a panel of Lecturers.

5. The formation of a Methodist and general musical reference library.

6. A bureau of advice on all matters connected with church music.

7. The holding of a Festival of Praise in connection with the annual conference of the Methodist Church held in July.

Subscriptions: 6/- (30p) per member per annum – payable in advance – this to include the twelve issues of 'The Choir' magazine.'

A report was submitted to the Methodist Conference in 1935 requesting its approval of the formation of MCMS. This appears to have been noted but full recognition of the Society by the Conference had to wait until 1948.

The MCMS conference soon became an annual event, although none was held during the Second World War period. Conferences were held at High Leigh (Hoddesdon), The Hayes (Swanwick) and Willersley Castle (Matlock). In the immediate post-war years a pattern was established of rehearsing and singing a major choral work over the weekend.

The involvement of young people in the presentation of worship has been much encouraged by the Society. In 1964 an annual summer school, initially Youth Makes Music (dance and drama were added later) was started. In 1982 the British Methodist Youth Choir (BMYC) was formed.

MCMS also had an involvement with the development and production of two books for use in worship – in 1969 'Hymns and Songs' and in 1983 'Hymns and Psalms'.

In this short historical account it is impossible to mention all the particular mile-stones but the following are some notable dates:

1970	First Bulletin published.
1974	MCMS incorporated into the Division of Ministries.
1984	First joint conference with Local Preachers.
1985	Golden Jubilee.
1990	First Ecumenical conference organised.

1991	District Music secretaries appointed by the Connexion.
1992	Methodist Conference inaugurated Commission of Music (report published in 1994).
1992	MCMS Library relocated to Wesley College Bristol.
1993	Organ Training Scheme launched.
1995	Diamond Jubilee with special service at Wesley's Chapel, London.
1998	Reorganisation of Methodism abolishes 'Divisions' and MCMS becomes independent of the Connexion.
1999	Creative Arts Forum in Methodism established with MCMS as a member.
2000	'Leading Music in Worship', a training resource, published by MCMS.
2003	MCMS registered as a charity.

Membership of MCMS has never reached 1,000. The following table illustrates membership trends:

1935	18	**1981**	818
1937	332	**1990**	941
1949	685	**1995**	858
1960	692	**2000**	692
1965	691	**2005**	538
1971	836	**2007**	494
1975	911	**2009**	453

At the turn of the 21st century concerns were beginning to be expressed about the future direction for MCMS and how it could become relevant to changing patterns and styles of worship. In May 2005 the Executive Committee met with a well known church consultant and trainer to discuss future possibilities for MCMS. After a wide ranging discussion the advice offered was that MCMS alone was too small to be able to meet its aspirations and it ought to give serious consideration to becoming part of a wider and more effective organisation. At roughly the same time changes were afoot within Methodism which resulted in the withdrawal of funding and support to a number of groups exploring and expressing creativity. In the light of this MCMS took a number of strategic decisions which are described in the final chapter of this book, which led ultimately to the creation of ArtServe and the transfer of the Society's activities to the new organisation.

Methodist Church Music Society

CANTATE DOMINO

1935 - 2010

Looking Back

Ronald Lander

The late Ronald F Lander, FRCO was associated with the MCMS at its inception. He served more than one term on its Executive Committee and was later made an Honorary Life Member of the Society. For many years he was Organist and Choirmaster at Spital St. Methodist Church, Dartford, Kent. He contributed this memoir to '1935–1995. Sixty Years of the Methodist Church Music Society', published to mark the Society's Diamond Jubilee in 1995. Despite the author's reflection of a point of view on music for worship which, though still held by some in the mid 1990s, may already seem dated only fifteen years later, the memoir is reproduced substantially as it was first published to record the author's personal reminiscences of some of the officers of the Society in its early years.

It is well-known that policemen are always getting younger, and I think that this must also be true of church musicians. I have formed this impression while I have been delving into my memories of the early days of the MCMS. My recollections of the 1930s, especially of the conference of 1934, which led to the founding of the society, are of elderly gentlemen in severely clerical attire or in the most sombre lounge-suits; and these recollections are supported by some early photographs. Names that remain as distant memories are such as Luke Wiseman, Russell Maltby, J Ernest Rattenbury and John Telford.

A little later came the two men who established our society more than any others. Dr Clifford Towlson (Chairman, 1939-1963), and Dr Francis Westbrook (Ministerial Secretary, 1945-1975) who are still held in great respect and affection by many of us.

Dr Towlson was Head of Woodhouse Grove School, Yorkshire, a person of considerable authority and held in great esteem. He guided the society with a gentle firmness, but I remember being on the receiving end of the magisterial brush-off when, as a youngster, I was brave enough to try and take part in an early discussion. He showed great knowledge of hymnology, particularly of Charles Wesley's hymns. 'God of unexampled grace' and 'Father of everlasting grace' were especially dear to him. In the latter hymn he always asked us to follow the last two verses through without a break between them.

Francis Westbrook was a remarkable man in every way, and we are not likely to see the like of him again. He had a deep Christian faith, an encyclopaedic knowledge of music, and a deeply-felt love of music which often reduced him to tears. For many years at our conferences, the highlight of every year was Francis's exposition of a standard choral work, and on occasions at the conclusion of his performance, he was so deeply moved that he was known to run out of the hall to avoid his embarrassment.

Another personal memory – on one occasion Dr Westbook sharply criticised me, in a hymn session, for introducing a dominant seventh into a dominant chord – which I strongly denied. (It made no difference to our mutual regard). But who would bother about such a thing today? Such was Francis's extreme punctiliousness. Even in matters of business, so intense was his thinking and feeling, that Dr Towlson used to tell us that he could feel the platform vibrating under his feet!

This is not to say that everything was always sweetness and light. There were other fine characters in the fifties and sixties, strong and independent minds, many of whom had grown up in the various branches of Methodism which united in 1932. Inevitably there were differences of opinion not always expressed gently. But they had great respect for each other. Names which are still warmly remembered include Arthur Rutter, Wilfred Wyatt, Ralph Rowntree, Arthur Gregory, and lastly John Farmer who established *Youth Makes Music.*

A final thought. The strong convictions of those early members of the society were focused on the high standards set around our new hymn book of 1933, and linked with the Methodist Union. Our targets were clearly identified – good hymns (especially those of Charles Wesley), strong tunes, dedicated and skilled musicians, and the involvement of every worshipper. Our minds were not complicated by other instruments, choruses, worship songs, etc.

In many ways our task is more difficult now. Our Society must be much wider in its scope than it used to be – to be inclusive rather than exclusive – or otherwise be left behind to a few purists on the sidelines. But we still can and must maintain the highest standards that are possible.

Memories of the Methodist Church Music Society

Bryan Spinney

I had always been interested in music and hymns - ever since, as a young boy, I wondered who was this 'Charles Wesley', whose name was splattered across *The Methodist Hymn Book*, newly published at that time! My first contact with the Methodist Church Music Society was around 1969. This came about through the publication of *Hymns & Songs* (the Supplement to the 1933 *Methodist Hymn Book*) and also through meeting Ronald Lander and his wife, Norah, who was a member at the Chelsfield church, near Orpington, of which I was then the minister.

Through the Landers I first attended the MCMS Annual Conferences, held alternately at High Leigh and Swanwick. At these my wife, Joy, and I were introduced to many people, who became and remained our friends, and to realms of church music and experiences of a quality of singing beyond anything we had known before. By this time *Hymns & Songs* had been published and the conferences gave opportunity to explore this and other hymnody.

The range of lectures on all aspects of church music enlarged our knowledge. Among the lecturers the name of John Rutter stays in my memory, but there has been a large and varied range of musicians whose lectures have widened and deepened our understanding of music in worship. We would have to admit that some of the speakers were more appealing than others. One erudite scholar, whose name (mercifully) escapes me, used to sit with a large pile of his notes before him. As the lecture proceeded, the sheets he had read got higher while those still to come got lower – not always at the speed some of his listeners would have liked! We were blessed with speakers such as Fred Pratt Green, Ivor Keys, John Bell, John Wilson, Caryl Micklem and many others. Some sessions involved singing and introduced members to new music, as well as giving the opportunity to sing some familiar material in a larger company than usual. The Sunday morning services included many excellent preachers who stimulated thought on the place of music in worship. An anthem, prepared the previous afternoon, would be included in the worship.

Another joy of the annual conference was the fellowship of the meal table. Members sat at long tables, about a dozen at each side. Those arriving last would have the task/privilege of serving the others from the pots and dishes delivered to the top end of the table. While the food was eaten and enjoyed, there was plenty of conversation – especially between those from distant places who met only once a year at the Conference.

It was not long before I was elected to the Committee responsible for the running of the Society and its events. At that time the Rev. Wilfrid Little was the editor of the Society's quarterly *Bulletin*. He was then a Supernumerary minister living in

Bristol and very knowledgeable about church music and hymnody. He had become the first editor of the *Bulletin* in 1970 and at a committee meeting in 1976 he commented that he was glad to say that no errors appeared in the *Bulletin*, - to which I replied that I had noticed several errors in the previous issue! If Wilfrid's statement was meant as a trap, I fell into it and found myself being elected as the next editor of the *Bulletin*! I undertook this responsibility for several years and this, again, brought me into touch with many people who enriched my knowledge and understanding of church music. My only previous experience of editing was a short-lived handwritten grammar school class magazine in the 1940s. After retirement I was for some years editor of a local community magazine, so my efforts for MCMS bore later fruit.

When I first became a member of the Society, the Rev. Francis Westbrook had recently retired from being the Committee Chairman. He had been involved with MCMS since its formation in 1935. His knowledge, experience and personality impressed and endeared him to the membership. He stepped down from office in 1968 and was succeeded by the Rev. Norman Goldhawk, whom I first knew as a tutor at Richmond College in the 1950s where I was in training for the ministry. It was a privilege and pleasure to renew acquaintance with him. He served as MCMS Committee Chairman from 1968 until 1983, there being no limit on the term of office at that time. He managed the Committee and led the Society in an exemplary style. The Society then thought fit to invite me to succeed him and so I served as Chairman from 1983-92.

The principal task was, of course, to chair the MCMS Committee. This consisted of people with considerable musical knowledge and experience – but there were at times differences of opinion and temperament - the functions of being chairman and referee sometimes overlapped! However, for the most part, people worked together harmoniously – as befits musicians. The Committee had two secretaries during my time as Editor and Chairman – the Rev. Ivor H. Jones, as Ministerial Secretary and Mr Ralph Bailey as Lay Secretary. Between them they made the necessary arrangements between meetings of the Committee for the efficient and smooth running of the Society. The autumn meetings were held at the home of Ralph and Kathleen Bailey in Cheltenham and were social as well as a business occasions, with good hospitality from our hosts. the Spring Committee meetings were held at Addington Palace, which at that time was the Headquarters of Royal School of Church Music. Dr. Lionel Dakers, the Principal, made us all very welcome and the overnight hospitality enabled us to claim that we had slept in a palace!

At times, the Chairman has to be the principal representative of the Society. In 1985 MCMS celebrated its Golden Jubilee with a service at Wesley's Chapel, London. It was my privilege to lead the service, the sermon being preached by the Rev. Dr. John A. Newton, and prayers of intercession led by the Rev. Norman Goldhawk. Jean Fryer and Miriam Ellis (members of the Society) read the lessons, and the organists were Ronald Thomson and Clifford Harman. I mention the organists because their role is often overlooked. I maintain (from experience!) that a service can be ruined more by a bad organist than by a bad preacher. Happily, the converse is equally true!

In 1988 the 250th anniversary of the Wesleys' conversion was celebrated. In this connection, there was an impressive service in St. Paul's cathedral attended by the Queen. My wife and I attended, representing MCMS. In this same year I was asked to devise a Festival of Praise entitled *How Great a Flame* incorporating the experience of John and the hymns of Charles. This also included one of John's translations from the German and hymns written by the Rev. Dr. Fred Pratt Green and the Rev. Brian Hoare. The prayers for this were compiled by the Rev. Norman Wallwork and this production was used in many places throughout the country as part of that year's celebration.

On another occasion I was privileged, as Chairman, to represent the Society at a celebratory festival of the Royal School of Church Music in the Albert Hall. The warm relationship between MCMS and RSCM has been beneficial in many ways. Lionel Dakers was a popular lecturer at MCMS conferences and in later years I was also privileged to represent MCMS at Lionel Dakers' funeral in Salisbury Cathedral.

Whilst MCMS was founded at the Connexional level, many Methodists Districts also had Music Committees on which members of the Society served. I had experience of these in the London South East, London South West, Bristol and Southampton Districts. These committees organised Festivals of Praise, performances of sacred music, talks on music in worship and generally tried to encourage and raise the musical standards of local churches. Among many uplifting experiences, I recall a performance of Fauré's *Requiem* conducted by Martin Ellis - I think it took place in the chapel of Charterhouse School. The choristers were drawn from various church choirs and congregations in the London South West District. Another such gathering in the Southampton District was a Festival of Praise held in the Southampton Central Hall, at which the Rev. Ray Short, much of whose ministry was with the BBC, was the presenter.

Through MCMS my wife and I have made and kept many personal friendships over the years. While it is always dangerous to name names for fear of omissions, we think of some of these – Pam and Philip Carter, who served as Conference Secretaries for many years; the late Ken Trickett whose knowledge of hymnody and church music seemed inexhaustible; Janet Taylor (Membership Secretary); and Dinah Smedley (Bookstall Manager).

MCMS was also, for me, the means of introduction to The Hymn Society. I was able to attend some of its annual conferences and am kept in touch by its informative (and often amusing) Bulletins. In an age when some of what is sung in our churches might be classed as 'vain repetitions', it is good to learn of modern hymns and their writers who are bringing deeper concepts and more poetic language into modern Christian hymnody.

I was also privileged to be a member of the Texts Sub-committee for the production of *Hymns & Psalms* under the chairmanship of the Rev. Ivor Jones. Our task was not to select which hymns should be included or omitted, but to consider carefully the precise form of wording of the hymns that the Main Hymnbook Committee had already selected. However there were a few instances where the Sub-committee suggested that the Main Committee should reconsider the inclusion of a hymn that either seemed too obscure or unsuitable for modern worship. Overall the task was fascinating because, thanks to past editing, some older hymns had acquired variant forms of wording. Our aim was to preserve as much as possible of the original, unless archaic wording obscured the meaning. We also reviewed the number and order of verses to be included. Many hymns are sung in an abbreviated version of their original form, e.g. '*O for a thousand tongues...*' had 18 verses. We had to be especially careful with the Wesley hymns because there is usually a train of thought linking each verse to the one following. We carefully considered, and sometimes moderated, the use of militaristic imagery and we also faced the inclusive language issue, In hymns written in the 20th century we considered whether 'thee' and 'thou' could be changed to 'you'. Of course if the term came at the end of a line, this might not be possible for rhyming reasons. The discussions between members at these meetings were a learning experience that benefited me in my understanding and use of hymns and their function in public worship.

Another personal consequence was a link with the Charles Wesley Society. No doubt it was my MCMS connection that led to an invitation to speak at their annual conference on the Wesleys' 1741 *Collection of Psalms and Hymns*. I must admit that this entailed intensive study to prepare, but, as the conference was held at Mansfield College, I can claim to have been an Oxford lecturer!

I look back on my quarter-century of active participation in the Methodist Music Society with great pleasure and gratitude for the ways in which my knowledge of church music in general, and hymnody in particular, has been enriched. This has had an effect upon the way in which I have led (and still lead) public worship in churches large and small. I am grateful to all those members of MCMS whose experience and friendship have enriched my own life and ministry over the past 40 years.

Charles Wesley and 'The Present Age'
Digest of a paper by Rev Arthur S Gregory, MA (1895-1989)

Andrew Pratt

Arthur Gregory was a member of the Committee which produced the 1933 Methodist Hymn Book and the author of its Companion, 'Praises with Understanding'. The original paper on which this digest is based was written for the Society in the late 1960's. The digest has been prepared by Andrew Pratt, who has added a substantial piece of his own work, reflecting on the place of Charles Wesley's hymns 40 years on from Gregory's original paper.

I

At a time when everything in the Church and out of it is shaken by forces we can neither measure nor control, it may be instructive to consider how things stand with Charles Wesley. For 200 years his hymns have given to Methodist worship its most distinctive trait, and for at least 100 years they have also claimed pride of place in almost every non-Methodist hymnal in the English language. If Watts may be accounted the real founder of the English hymn, Wesley continues to outnumber him in every collection save the Congregational.

The point at issue is whether verses written in the language and uttering the thoughts of the eighteenth century can serve the religious needs of the late twentieth. In 1762 Wesley made a paraphrase of Leviticus 8:35, *Keep the charge of the Lord, that ye die not* – the 'charge' referring to some Tabernacle ceremonial. In Wesley's stanza it embodies the commitment of every Christian to *'serve the present age'* (MHB 578). How far, in fact, can Charles Wesley serve the present age; and in particular, 'the present age'-group of under 30s?

The first thing to be said is that our question can only be understood in the context of the whole breakdown of communication between church and community. It is not simply a matter of whether today we want to sing *If so poor a worm as I* and *Save me, gasping at Thy feet* and *Esteem the scandal of the cross* and *only seek divine applause* and so on.

The heart of the problem lies much deeper. How much longer, with the coming of the non-church, will the traditional idiom of Christian piety continue to serve us? The archaisms of Charles Wesley are not noticeably more out of key than those of all hymns and prayers of the past. The question of how far it is right to limit the literary forms of worship to contemporary language is claiming the attention of the whole church, and the answer is by no means agreed on or even in sight. It must not be forgotten that an unfamiliar note in the language of worship may itself be a help as well as a hindrance, by preserving the sense of 'otherness' which is one, if not the only, essential element in worship.

But with this larger issue in mind what is to be said of these 250 hymns by one eighteenth century author which still occupy one quarter of the entire space in the (1933) Methodist Hymn Book? This number will prove to be out of all proportion to their present and future usefulness. There is simply not room in any viable future hymn book for anything approaching so many.

Such considerations in no degree impair, indeed they enhance, the greatness of Charles Wesley in his own day and, through his hymns, in ours also. All Wesley's hymns, including the popular *Hark! the herald-angels sing* are packed with the most uncompromising affirmations of Christian doctrine. If that in itself makes them unacceptable to 'the present age', they share the reproach with *O come, all ye faithful,* the creeds, the sacraments, the Lord's Prayer itself.

II
(1) Use of Wesley's hymns within Methodism

The total number of hymns by Charles Wesley in the MHB is 243. Of these:
- About 50 are in constant use everywhere.
- About 60 others are sung regularly, but less frequently than the above, and by no means everywhere.
- Some 40-50 more are used very occasionally.
- Of the remaining 80 hymns, the great majority are never sung. In some few cases this is because the tune set is unknown or unsuitable.

By way of comparison, the current American Methodist Hymnal, published in 1964, contains 72 Charles Wesley hymns out of 550, or 13% as against the 25% in the Methodist Hymn Book.

(2) Use of Wesley's hymns outside Methodism

It is surely significant that nine non-Methodist English hymn books at present in use contain between them no fewer than 60 hymns by Charles Wesley. Some 20 of these are in every collection. *Congregational Praise,* published in 1951, has the highest total (45) and proportion (nearly 6%); this includes some sixteen which have escaped all other editors. Against this the Presbyterian book shows only 3% – suggesting, perhaps, that Isaac Watts's affinity with Charles Wesley is greater than that of the Scottish paraphrases!

There are, of course, historical reasons why British Methodists should still be singing more than four times as many of Charles Wesley's hymns than anybody else. But should so great a disparity be permanent? It is, to say the least, matter for regret that some of the very greatest hymns in the English language, e.g. *Let earth and heaven combine* and *Author of faith, eternal Word* should be entirely unknown outside the covers of one denominational hymn book. All are at once plain, profound and singable. Perhaps it is permissible to express the hope that the introduction of fellow Christians to hymns of this calibre may be opened to British Methodists by church reunion.

III

The word 'singable' compels a brief reference to hymn tunes. Charles Wesley had a strong sense of rhythm and a genuine gift of music, if not the genius of his two famous sons; and most of his favourite metres are eminently singable – especially S.M. and 4-line 7s. There is, unfortunately, one exception, namely 6-line 8s. This metre, in which many of the great hymns of faith are written, is a constant difficulty and is, perhaps on its way out. MHB has no fewer than 6% of its tunes in this metre: the BBC hymnal is down to 2.2%. A limited supply of excellent tunes is available; but congregations too often fail on the concentration and effort they call for. Far too many 6/8 tunes are either dull or else too florid – in the jolly 'early Methodist' manner.

Many of us are only partially aware that if WILTON is too brash and brassy for Wesley's masterpiece of devotion *O Thou who camest from above*, our habitual treatment of *And can it be* (to SAGINA) is unworthy if not a disgrace. LANSDOWN and – even better – HOLY FAITH are available; but we continue to miss much of Wesley's realisation of amazing love and ineffable mystery in a rollicking enjoyment more proper to swings and roundabouts. There is, of course, no final answer to these problems of musical fitness. Part of the privilege and duty of the MCMS, and those who share its ideals, is to continue seeking, and then commending, the most worthy manner of praise. One or two good modern tunes are at hand; for example, W K Stanton's ST MAWES, set in the BBC Hymn Book to *Come let us with our Lord arise*. It is becoming clear that the attempt to buy favour for the traditional hymns by marrying them to the most up-to-the-minute of popular melodies is mistaken, however well-intentioned. Music must match and interpret the thought of the hymn's writer. It must never try to be jam to his pill.

IV

In the final analysis, it has to be recognised that most of the criticism of Charles Wesley as 'irrelevant to the modem age' is simply part of the ever present offence of the Cross. His relevance or irrelevance is that of the Gospel. 'The great bulk of his hymns', says the Anglican C S Phillips, 'have, of course, sunk beneath the stream of time beyond all possibility of rescue ... but if ever the glow of the early Methodist comes back to the English speaking world, men will find no hymns more fitted to express it than the best of what Charles Wesley has bequeathed to them'. Indeed, the present climate of theological thinking exhibits certain factors which should make Charles Wesley more, rather than less, congenial to our own century:

- his intense interest in personal, individual experience ranges him on the side of all who in our day stand for personal fulfilment and freedom.

- Wesley has much to say about the holiness of work – *'my hallowed labour'* – *'this humble work of mine'*. The holiness of play is not other: 'the secular life regarded as a means of grace' (Dr Rattenbury's phrase about this aspect of Wesley's teaching) is entirely in tune with all that the most 'with-it' exponents of the new evangelism have to say about communication and development. There may even be some affinity between pop art and 'dancing at the sound of His name'.

- the all-embracing universality of Charles Wesley's appeal is entirely germane to a world view in which the unity of the human race is the dominant, over-riding condition of every human endeavour.

One special claim to present relevance must not be overlooked. Charles Wesley was not only an evangelist, he was also a churchman. His loyalty to the Church was fed and realised most fully and richly in the fellowship of the Methodist societies for which his hymns were primarily written – not for the formal worship of the Church. But the eucharistic hymns, 166 of them, have a distinct bearing upon the problems of churchmanship today. They remind us first of all of the mutual interdependence of evangelism and sacramental observance and they are well fitted to the now generally agreed view that the people should be given more opportunity to share vocally in the sacrament. One of these hymns, never used since the eighteenth century, found its way as recently as 1957 into a modem hymn book. It begins:

> *Jesu, my Lord and God, bestow*
> *All which Thy sacrament doth show*

and ends with the prayer:

> *Only do Thou my heart prepare*
> *To find Thy real presence there*
> *And all Thy fulness gain.*

In many of these hymns Charles Wesley points clearly to the realisation of all the present hopes and strivings of Christians of every name.

This paper began by suggesting that behind all discussion of the 'relevance' of Charles Wesley lies the larger question of how far succeeding generations of Christians are likely to sing hymns at all. If they do – and surely the hymn is uniquely fitted to give every member a part of the Church's offering of praise – it seems certain that fifty at least of Wesley's hymns will continue into a third century of service to English speaking Christians. A drastic reduction, but 'the present age' is most exactly their proper field of influence. Their word is for all, in this or any age, who have ears and hearts to hear and voices to sing.

■■

F ollowing[1] the 300th anniversary of the birth of Charles Wesley (2007) it is appropriate to reflect on how near Arthur Gregory was in his estimation of the value and use of the hymns in the light of what has followed.

Gregory anticipated a continuing decline in the use of Charles Wesley's texts though the decline has not been as steep as he estimated, some 156 texts appearing in *Hymns & Psalms*, less than 25% of the total. When the next collection of Methodist hymns, *Singing Our Faith* is published this will have reduced to 80, around 10% of the total content of the collection, and this is more than had been submitted for scrutiny following the Conference of 2009. The decline in their use in American hymnals has been less sharp.

As Gregory had noticed the language of much of Wesley's writing was becoming less than intelligible. His argument that its obscurity adds to something of the mystery that we associate with religion is untenable in the 21st century, though some will still concur with it. The key themes to which Wesley gave expression are obviously there in his corpus and it has been easier for Methodist editors to stay with 'what is safe' rather than look for new interpretations of these themes or to commission them from contemporary authors. In saying this I am making the case that the use of many, though not all, Wesley hymns has been extended longer than might otherwise have been the case had the hymns been assessed on their intelligibility and singability. That is not to undervalue the texts, but to say that they have their own intrinsic excellence, yet that excellence is set in a language and culture remote from our own and even more detached from those among whom we seek to mission. At best Wesley was the Milton of hymnody, but Milton is not our contemporary; his language and allusions require commentary and explanation. So do those of Wesley's hymns.

If all of this is accepted how do we assess these hymns today? Their power is less now in their continued use, than in the influence Charles Wesley has had through them on other writers.

It is with Wesley that we find the first true exploration of hymns which interpret and enable the memorisation not just of scripture, but of theology derived from it. For this to work it is necessary for an author to know scripture, to reflect on it and to adopt or formulate theology and then, in addition, to give expression to this theology in the form of poetry that can be sung. It is in this art that Charles Wesley demonstrated consummate skill. There are still authors today who paraphrase texts having neither the inclination, or perhaps the skill, to follow Wesley's example. Yet there are those who follow in his footsteps.

---

[1]Some of what follows was first published in a chapter entitled, 'The Influence of Charles Wesley on Contemporary Hymnody' in Newport.K., 2007, *Charles Wesley: Life. Literature. Legacy*, SCM.

This influence is more subtle, but nonetheless significant.[2] For example, a hymn in the classic style of Charles Wesley in every respect is provided by Brian Wren. *'Great God, your love has called us here'.*[3] It uses the same metre and rhyme scheme as *'Behold the servant of the Lord'* (in which some 42 scriptural references have been noted). The text is eclectic in its use of scriptural references, gospels and Pauline epistles being prominent, but the Old Testament also features, *'... you call our name,/and then receive us as your own'* (Isaiah 43:1). The overall theme is that of sin and redemption and the thrust of the text is clearly Arminian for it is the purpose of God in Christ to

> *...show how grandly love intends*
> *to work till all creation sings,*
> *to fill all worlds, to crown all things.*

Notice the repetition of the word 'all'. There is even an echo of *'And can it be'* as Wren understands that we are *'...half bound by inner chains'* while Wesley has the subject of his text *'fast bound by sin and nature's night'* and, within the same stanza announces, *'My chains fell off'.* In passing it is worth noting Wren's text in *Hymns & Psalms* is set to Eric Routley's ABINGDON, a tune originally composed for *'And can it be'* – a further seeking after a suitable tune for these words that Gregory noted in this article. Ultimately Wren concludes that *'...love is making all things new'*, a sentiment which is not far from that of Charles Wesley in *'Love divine all loves excelling'*: *'Changed from glory into glory,/Till in heaven we take our place'.*[4]

Timothy Dudley-Smith's *'Child of the stable's secret birth'*[5] mirrors *'Let earth and heaven combine'.* Both texts compare and contrast the human child Jesus with God the creator and Lord of all. In this there is nothing particularly unusual. Graham Kendrick's popular text, *'From heaven you came'* (*'The Servant King'*), does just this. For Dudley-Smith the *'Child of the stable's secret birth*' is *'The Lord by right of the Lords of earth'.* This is the same God who Wesley says, *'Laid his glory by'*, *'Our God contracted to a span,/Incomprehensibly made man'.* Dudley-Smith puts it this way the *'Voice that rang through the courts on high/contracted now to a wordless cry'.* The only other use of the word 'contracted' in English hymnody in this sense is in Charles Wesley's older brother, Samuel's, 'Hymn to God the Son'.

In both these authors, Wren and Dudley-Smith, we recognise the debt which is owed to Charles Wesley in the use of scripture, the logic of form, the strictness of

---

[2] What follows here is drawn from my essay 'The influence of Charles Wesley on Contemporary hymnody' which was published in *Charles Wesley Life, Literature and Legacy*, Newport, K.G.C. and Campbell T.A., Epworth, 2007, p393-413.
[3] *Hymns & Psalms* No. 500, but listed as 'Lord God, your love has called us here'.
[4] 'Love divine all loves excelling'
[5] *Hymns & Psalms*, No. 124

rhyme and the imperative to provide theological interpretation. The same could be said of other authors. The influence continues.

Teresa Berger has noted that the hymns of Charles Wesley carried with them particular emphases, that of salvation specifically, the experience of salvation and the understanding of revelation, the experience of salvation as realised eschatology and the struggle for Christian perfection.[6] These themes can again be traced in the writing of authors from the end of the 20th and the beginning of the 21st centuries.

1. The Emphasis on Salvation

The language of Martin E Leckebusch's 'A crown of piercing thorns'[7] is characteristic of the realism that was beginning to show itself in much hymnody at the end of the twentieth century.[8] Yet the individual nature of the writing and the sense of salvation being with a purpose,

> Your feet they firmly held
> as nails were hammered through:
> my feet are free-but how can I
> not choose to follow you?

echoes Charles Wesley, 'Died he for me'? ... 'I rose, went forth, and followed thee'.[9] What is lacking is the wider vision that drove Charles Wesley's imperative for evangelism. Hayward Osbourne's communion hymn takes a further step in stating that

> As the bread is broken
> Let each of us recall
> The person who was broken
> Because he loved us all.[10]

There is here a flavour of Arminianism that must be present in any soteriological text if it is to be identified as having been influenced by Charles Wesley. Carl Daw Jr's 'How shallow former shadows seem'[11] describes the reality of the cross and admits that 'with awe we glimpse its true import/ and dare to call it good'. The text is inclusive in its tenor.

A step closer to Wesley is provided in Fred Pratt Green's 'Life has many rhythms, every heart its beat'.[12] The third stanza is particularly pertinent:

---

[6] Berger, T., 1995, *Theology in Hymns?* Kingswood, Nashville, p.107-153.
[7] Leckebusch, M.E., *More than words*, Kevin Mayhew, Stowmarket, 2000, No.3.
[8] See especially 'These things did Thomas count as real', Troeger, T., Doran, C., *New Hymns for the Lectionary*, Oxford University Press, New York, 1986, p.68
[9] *Hymns & Psalms*, 216.
[10] Osbourne, H in *Living Lord*, Joseph Weinberger, London, 1979.
[11] Daw, C.P. Jr., *A Year of Grace*, Hope Publishing Company Ltd., Illinois, 1990
[12] *Hymns & Songs*, Methodist Publishing House, London, 1969, No.85.

It was you who promised: All who seek shall find.
What we find lies deeper than our reach of mind;
What we found was you, Lord, you the God Above.
You had come as Victim to the world you love.

It is clear that the victim is the Jesus of the cross and the salvation inherent here is for all. The sense of being saved for a purpose is underlined by the last line of the hymn: *'ours the only victory we would serve and share'.* Culturally speaking the latter half of the twentieth century was a time of increasing individualism. Many of the hymns and spiritual songs of this time lack Wesley's understanding of fellowship and the inclusivity which he had promulgated. There was, nevertheless, a reaction against this mood. It is to Pratt Green again that we turn for words of simplicity and elegance. The cross is assumed and the acceptance of incorporation of the church within the cross is stated. Amid change *'The Church of Christ in every age'*[13] must *'keep on rising from the dead'.* As the text develops it is clear that the gospel is something which is both practical and universal. It is to reach the victims of injustice around the world. The 'cure of souls' is found in the shed blood of Christ and the role of the saved is to

> *... have no mission but to serve*
> *In full obedience to our Lord:*
> *To care for all, without reserve,*
> *And spread his liberating Word.*

The word 'all' is significant and provides a validation of the Wesleyan soteriological influence within the hymn.

It is clear from this brief summary that the combination of a soteriology with an Arminian theology is not as obvious in late twentieth century hymn writers as it had been in the texts of Charles Wesley. The influence can be detected in Methodist writers, but it is not their primary theme.

2. The Experience of Salvation and the Understanding of Revelation

For Charles Wesley the means of salvation is disclosed in scripture. God enables that revelation to be understood and interpreted as well as being its source. *'Come, Holy Ghost, our hearts inspire'* asks that the Holy Ghost should *'unseal the sacred book'* while acknowledging that *'moved by thee /The prophets wrote and spoke'.*

George W. Briggs's *'God has spoken by his prophets'* states that *'God is speaking by his spirit'...In the age-long word expounding /God's own message, now as then'.* So while there is a rooting in history there is a new interpretation for every age.

---

[13] Green, F. Pratt, *Twenty-six Hymns*, Epworth/Methodist Publishing House, London, 1971.

Michael Forster in *'The Saviour of the nations'* states unequivocally

> *The mystery of ages,*
> *the secret long-concealed,*
> *of full and free salvation,*
> *at last has been revealed.*

And it is clear from the context that this revelation is in the birth of Christ.

Brian Wren takes a step further. Salvation is seen as revealed in the love of God seen in Christ, clearly visible in scripture, but it is still working *'when a hungry child is fed'.*[14]

3. The Experience of Salvation as Realised Eschatology

Salvation now is a theme which would be expected to be emphasised in an age when everything is instant. The constant search for opportunities in, and solutions for, the context in which we find ourselves as human beings are common preoccupations. Such opportunities have to be a present reality or they are disregarded as irrelevant. We seek to 'serve the present age' but we also require our eschatological ends to be met within its compass.

Christopher Idle takes Romans 12 as a starting point for his text *'Now in view of all God's mercies'.* He begins with an interpretation of the scripture, recognising all that has gone before that has ensured the redemption of the Christian. It then becomes clear that in the light of this redemption the individual should be committed to service so that Christians might

> *laugh and cry with one another*
> *through the joy or pain God sends;*
> *welcome neighbour, sister, brother,*
> *giving time and making friends.*

The actions of God in which the believer shares are seen as being necessary and possible now. We do not need to wait for some future moment to bring in the reign of God. Through faith and action its reality can be experienced now:

> *See the rule of Christ advancing,*
> *let his will be understood;*
> *praying, working, peace-enhancing,*
> *evil overcome with good.*

---

[14] 'There's a spirit in the air', *Hymns & Psalms* No. 326.

4. The Struggle for Christian Perfection

If any theme defined Charles Wesley's approach to religion it was the struggle for Christian perfection. Most recently this has been underlined by the publication of the definitive edition of Charles Wesley's sermons. Charles Wesley struggled to achieve perfection and saw this as the right activity for the Christian under God's grace in the power of the spirit.

Brian Foley's text expresses in very simple language what Charles Wesley believed, that

> *The Law of God is no mere list*
> *of things to do and not to do,*
> *but God's perfection - this alone*
> *the yes and no of what we do!*

In this perspective

> *The Will of God must be our will,*
> *to wish, to want, to do, to be;*
> *and with the mind of God, to think,*
> *and through the eyes of God to see!*

What is lacking here is the rigorous self examination and introspection which was so characteristic of Charles Wesley's personal religion, the *'sensibility of sin, [the] pain to feel it near'.* For David G. Preston, echoing Psalm 15, the righteous are those who are *'..pure in heart, whose spotless lives/ By word and deed obey your will'.* This is nearer to Wesley though cannot claim to have been influenced by him.

'In judgment, Lord, arise' by Timothy Dudley-Smith asks,
> *Discern my thoughts, I pray,*
> *Discover all my mind*
> *And keep me in the narrow way*
> *To innocence inclined.*

In these words, written in 1998, though sounding as though they come from an earlier phase in Smith's writing, there is an echo of Psalm 26 yet it can be argued that here he is very near to that sense of introspection that we have observed in Charles Wesley.

In conclusion

The use of Charles Wesley's hymns has diminished. Some hymns are retained because they are familiar and are thus helpful as a reminder of the faith which has formed us. Others are of historic significance, though less likely to be sung. While we see fewer of Charles Wesley's hymns in hymnals, the influence of his writing continues both here and throughout the world.

'Singing the Faith'

By happy coincidence, some key milestones in the history of MCMS have coincided with the publication of new collections of hymns for the people called Methodist. MCMS began when the 1933 Methodist Hymn Book was being introduced; it completes its transformation into ArtServe as the church looks forward to a comprehensive new collection of Hymns and Songs to support Methodist worship in the early years of the 21st Century. **Barbara Bircumshaw** *and Editor in Chief* **Peter Brophy** *describe the background to the new collection and outline the policies adopted in compiling it.*

The Methodist Conference set up a Music Resources Group (MRG) in 2004 and directed it to produce a supplement to *Hymns and Psalms* in collaboration with the Methodist Publishing House. However the purpose of the MRG was widened considerably at the 2007 Conference when the Group was authorised to prepare a new 'baseline' collection of authorised hymns and songs in succession to *Hymns and Psalms*. Subsequently the work of the MRG has been resourced by the Connexional Team. The 2009 Conference further endorsed the publication of a new collection.

MRG believes that a new hymnbook can provide the Methodist Church in the twenty-first century with a resource for the worship of God that celebrates our Methodist heritage and contains the best of contemporary hymnody. Singing the faith has been at the heart of the Methodist story from its beginnings. Our history and experience bear witness to the power of music in worship. It speaks to our hearts, comforts, encourages, challenges and inspires us on our Christian journey.

It is nearly thirty years since *Hymns and Psalms* was published and since that time there has been an explosion in the material written to be sung in worship. As well as a vast increase in quantity, there has also been an increase in the diversity of style, both in terms of the words and the music. These include contemporary hymns and songs from Iona, Taizé and the world church. In addition there has been a commercialisation of worship music, with songs being promoted on CD's and DVD's as well as in print.

There were those who advocated that only an electronic resource should be produced. But the MRG has consistently believed that a printed resource is essential, to be used in churches without projection facilities, to be available to musicians, preachers and worship leaders and to those whose impairment necessitates a printed copy. Furthermore copyright restrictions can limit the material used electronically. The Group has also envisaged the hymnbook being used for private devotion as well as for public worship.

The members of the MRG have worked with commitment and enthusiasm to provide a rich collection for Christian worship which expresses the core beliefs of the Christian faith; reflects distinctive Methodist emphases and takes account of a range of musical styles. They have examined literally thousands of texts and considered them carefully in accordance with the criteria agreed by the 2009 Conference. The material has been subject to analysis in terms of balance, including genre, hymns to and about God, gender balance, theories of the atonement and material for children and young people.

Each item chosen by the MRG has also been scrutinised by the Faith and Order Committee so that the MRG and the Faith and Order Committee were of one mind when the final list was brought to the 2010 Conference for authorisation.

The collection contains over eight hundred hymns and songs. There is a section of liturgical settings and sung responses and the book concludes with a selection of canticles and psalms. The canticles will be similar to those in *Hymns and Psalms* and the psalms have been selected on the basis of their use within the liturgy and the lectionary. It is also hoped to provide an electronic resource for the words of hymns for which there is copyright clearance.

Alongside the process of deciding the content of the hymnbook the MRG Music Group has been working on musical arrangements. It has evaluated the musical settings of all the items in the collection. The general criterion of the Group has been to ensure that material is suitable for congregational singing and that tunes are accessible to musicians of varying abilities while maintaining the integrity of the original composition. A selection of descants have been provided, many new arrangements of modern hymns and songs to make them more accessible to both musicians and congregations and new tunes have been commissioned.

The full music edition will contain a comprehensive set of indexes similar to those printed in *Hymns and Psalms*. A fuller list of indexes will be available through the Rolling Resource, renamed *Singing the Faith Plus*. This electronic resource will be a free tool to internet users through the Methodist Church website and is intended to be a single point of access for information on Methodist hymns and worship. It is seen as an important facility providing information and support to hymnbook users and should be available at the same time as the launch of the new collection.

Conference agreed to the Rolling Resource as 'a means of supplementing the core collection with contemporary hymns and songs, some of which may be of a more ephemeral nature' (MRG Report 2009). Texts of new material will be signposted regarding their source unless writers have given permission for their hymn or song to be viewed in full. It is hoped that the resource will be able to show-case talent particularly Methodist writers and there might be those willing to share their material in order to make it known.

A considerable number of people have given of their time, their skills and musical expertise voluntarily to prepare the collection and it has been a long journey. But Conference has now authorised *Singing the Faith* to be published in 2011 and we look forward to a new chapter in the history of Methodist hymnody with its launch at 2011 Conference.

Passing the Baton

Godfrey Talford

Changing Perspectives

In 2010 and coinciding with the Society's 75th anniversary, the work of the Methodist Church Music Society took a dramatic new direction; it transformed itself into ArtServe, an organisation committed to supporting practitioners of all the creative arts in worship. It thus responded to changes in patterns of worship since Methodist Union in the 1930s and the increasing recognition of the role creative arts other than music play in worship.

Creative arts have long been used as a means for expressing and communicating spirituality and theology. There is a general awareness that great pieces of art and performance such as Wren's church buildings, Michelangelo's paintings, Handel's Messiah or the Oberammergau Passion Play can have a significant impact on faith and the understanding of the Gospel. Methodism has always understood the potential impact of the arts; the preface to the Methodist Hymn Book (1933) asserts that 'Methodism was born in song' and that tradition of music and hymnody has been developed, not only through the work of the Methodist Church Music Society, but also the National Methodist Youth Brass Band; the British Methodist Youth Choir and the Methodist Association of Youth Clubs (MAYC) Orchestra and Singers.

During the 1960s and 1970s artistic disciplines other than music began to feature more widely in worship, arising from an increasing awareness of the role of the arts in society. The arts became more accessible to all. More and more artistic disciplines such as dance, drama and the visual arts began to enhance worship alongside music at a local level. The Methodist Church played its part in supporting these developments through initiatives such as the establishment of 'The Methodist Church Collection of Modern Christian Art' and 'Youth Makes Music, Dance and Drama'.

Changing structures

The 1990s was a time of change within the structures of the Methodist Church in Great Britain. The period saw the establishment of the ministry of Worship Leaders within the local church to support preachers. In carrying out their ministry Worship Leaders are called upon to lead worship that uses the arts and technology (as appropriate and as available) to communicate the Good News and to present God's Word with creativity and imagination.

Reorganisation of the various 'Divisions' in the structures of the Methodist Church in Great Britain led to the establishment of the MCMS as an independent group outside the Connexion. At the same time the Conference recognised the role the creative arts can potentially play in the life of the Church through the establishment of the Forum for Creative Arts in Methodism comprising representatives from across the various artistic disciplines as well as members of the Connexional Team. The Forum's aims were:

- To affirm the creative arts in the life of the Church
  - ❖ as an aid to worship
  - ❖ as a tool for mission
  - ❖ as important for personal and corporate wholeness
- To develop local churches' appreciation of the creative arts
- To help people use their creative gifts
- To act as a resource for those leading worship, retreats, etc
- To be aware of the cultural life of our society, and consider how Methodism might make a contribution to it.

In addition, a member of the Connexional Team was designated as a part time Co-ordinator of Creative Arts in Methodism and a number of Creative Arts volunteers were identified to head up work in particular disciplines.

However, in the Spring of 2005, against the background of declining church membership and ever more stringent financial constraints, the Methodist Council decided to discontinue financial support from central funds for the Church's creative arts work. This included removing the posts of Creative Arts Co-ordinator and the MAYC Communications and Creative Arts (Youth) Development Worker which, respectively, supported the Creative Arts Forum and creative arts work with young people. The Council expressed the hope that this work might become self-sustaining, with the help of Methodist Districts and others.

Following the announcement of the Methodist Council's decision, a group drawn from those working within the creative arts and concerned individuals met to explore possible ways forward to support the development and funding of the creative arts locally, across the Connexion and ecumenically. The conclusion of those discussions was a motion to the Methodist Conference proposing the creation of a separate Creative Arts Agency operating across the Connexion. Although the motion received approval from Conference it did not prove possible to turn that approval into practical action.

A New Initiative

Following the lack of progress on a Creative Arts Agency, the Methodist Church Music Society reaffirmed its commitment to the creation of a new organisation covering the creative arts in worship. The result of this commitment was the creation by MCMS of Methodist Arts Limited, a charitable limited company operating under the name of ArtServe. The Charity's object is to advance education for the public benefit in the use of creative arts in Christian worship.

The Charity has powers to further its object by:

- Initiating, supporting and sustaining the training and development of participants in all creative arts contributing to public worship in the Methodist Church;
- Initiating and supporting the development of resources and materials to assist the use of creative arts in worship, mission and spiritual growth;
- Supporting initiatives in creative arts in co-operation with other churches having objects similar to those held by the Methodist Church or Local Ecumenical Partnerships that include Methodists; and
- Supporting and promoting creative arts activities undertaken by other organisations whose objects are not inconsistent with those of the Methodist Church.

ArtServe began to work in parallel with MCMS in 2008, and its initial Trustees and Officers were appointed by, and largely drawn from, those of MCMS It committed itself to work, either on its own or in partnership with others, to:

- encourage and develop the use of all creative art forms which contribute to the life of the church;
- enable active participants in the arts, at all levels, to develop their skills and talents; and
- publicise and support initiatives by other organisations which contribute to the fulfilment of the objects of ArtServe.

ArtServe continues the work of MCMS in seeking to uphold and develop all aspects of the Church's musical life – whether it be worship bands, music groups, choirs, instrumentalists, organists or those who write hymns or worship songs. But worship increasingly includes performance arts such as dance, drama and mime in a variety of ways, and ArtServe encourages and supports the users of these art forms.

Visual arts also provide ever-expanding possibilities. In addition to the floral arts, banners, paintings and sculpture, there is increasing scope for innovative use of electronic media. ArtServe seeks to develop ways to make all these art forms more accessible to everyone for use in worship.

The Methodist Church Music Society agreed that ArtServe should become the public vehicle for its activities from 2009 and initially envisaged full integration within three years. In the light of the widespread acclaim which greeted the launch of ArtServe and the wastefulness of maintaining two parallel organisations with similar objectives, it was decided to bring forward the target date for the full integration of the Society into ArtServe to August 2010.

Thus the Society has adopted a structure fit for purpose in the 21st century and widened its objects to meet 21st century expectations in relation to worship. Whilst treasuring its heritage, it seeks to be responsive to change and to encourage innovation in using the skills and resources available to support newly emerging patterns of worship.

With acknowledgments to ArtServe's initial business plan, substantially drafted by Alistair Kennard after consultation with the other founding Trustees.